# I Know That!

# Touching

### Claire Llewellyn

W
## FRANKLIN WATTS
#### LONDON • SYDNEY

First published in 2004 by Franklin Watts
96 Leonard Street, London EC2A 4XD

Franklin Watts Australia
45-51 Huntley Street
Alexandria, NSW 2015

Text copyright © Claire Llewellyn 2004
Design and concept © Franklin Watts 2004

Series advisers: Gill Matthews, non-fiction literacy
    consultant and Inset trainer
Editor: Rachel Cooke
Series design: Peter Scoulding
Designer: James Marks
Photography: Ray Moller unless otherwise credited
Acknowledgements: Fritz Pölking/Ecoscene: 13tr. H Rogers/Trip: 21cl.
Paul Seheult/Eye Ubiquitous: 17bl. B. Stein/Still Pictures: 17tr.
Erika Stone/Still Pictures: 7. Cal Vornberger/Still Pictures: 15tr.
Thanks to our models, including Vanessa Dang, Sophie Hall, Latifah Harris,
Thomas Howe, Amelia Menicou, Spencer Mulchay and Ishar Sehgal.

A CIP catalogue record for this book is available from the British Library.

ISBN: 0 7496 5725 1

Printed in Malaysia

# Contents

# Touch and feel

Every day we touch things. Touching lets us feel the world around us. Touching is one of our senses.

▶ *We touch things with our hands and feet…*

and every part
of our body.

We have five
senses. They are
seeing, hearing,
tasting, smelling
and touching.

# Our skin

We touch things with our skin. We have skin all over our body.

▼ *Skin can be different colours.*

6

▲ *Our skin changes as we get older.*

Have a look at the skin on your face, hands, knees, elbows, and under your feet. Does it look and feel the same all over?

# What does it feel like?

Feeling something tells us about its shape, and whether it is smooth or rough.

▶ *This ball is round and smooth.*

▼ *This log is long and rough.*

Touching tells us lots of other things as well.

▶ *This teddy feels soft and furry.*

◀ *This dough feels sticky and squashy.*

Collect some toys to touch and feel. Tell a friend about each one's shape and how it feels.

9

# Feel the difference

▶ *Light*

We can feel if things are heavy or light.

▶ *Heavy*

We can feel if they are hot or cold.

► *Cold*

▲ *Hot*

We can feel if they are wet or dry.

► *Wet*

◄ *Dry*

How does a towel feel after you have used it to dry your hair?

# Feeling the air

Our skin feels the air around us.

▲ *We feel the air moving.*

*We feel if the air is hot…*

Birds feel the air as they fly. They often glide on moving air.

*or cold.*

13

# Good at feeling

Some parts of our body are good at feeling.

▶ *Our fingers can find a bead lost in the carpet.*

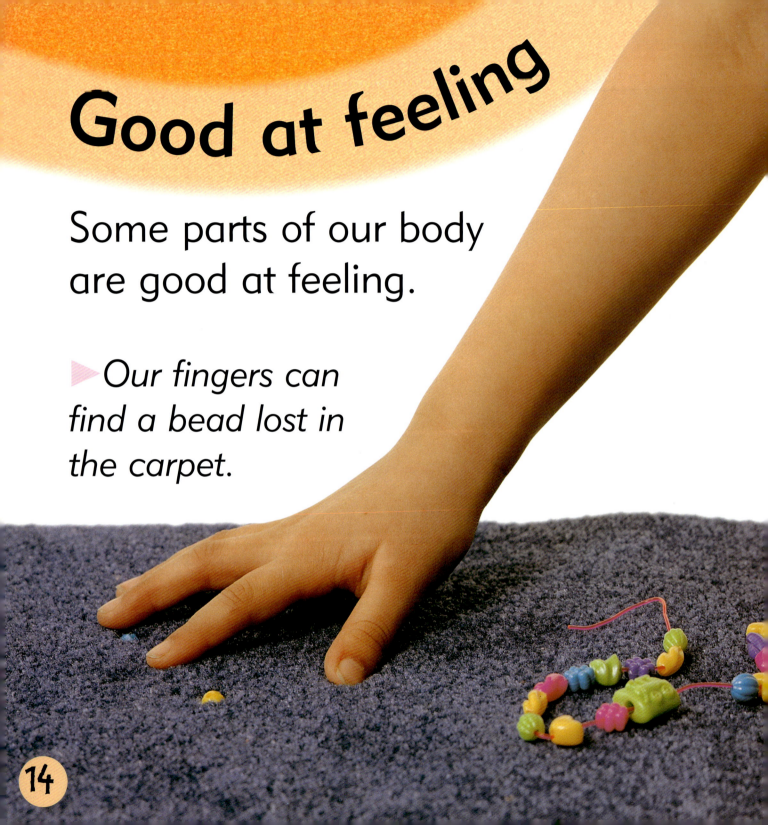

*Our feet feel a tiny pebble in the sand.*

A sea bird uses its beak to feel for food under the sand.

*Our tongue feels the tiny pips hidden in grapes.*

15

# Feeling our way

Our sense of touch is very useful when we cannot see.

▶ *We use our hands to feel our way when we cannot see.*

*Blind people see very badly or not at all. They sometimes use a stick to feel their way around.*

Moles cannot see well. They find their way using their nose and whiskers.

# Keeping safe

Touching and feeling help to keep us safe. They warn us about things that can hurt us.

►*Ow! That hot dish could burn me.*

What do you do when you touch something very hot?

▲ *Ow! These sharp stones could cut my feet.*

◄*Ow! My tooth hurts. I must go to the dentist.*

19

# A world of touch

Our sense of touch helps us to enjoy the world.

▶ *We all enjoy touching the people we love.*

*A baby rabbit feels soft and warm.*

Think about the things you like to touch. Why do you like them?

*A warm bed feels very cosy.*

# I know that...

**1** We touch things to feel the world around us.

**2** Touching is one of our body's senses.

**3** We touch things with our skin. It covers every part of our body.

**4** Feeling tells us a lot about things.

**5** Our skin feels moving air. It feels if things are warm or cold.

**6** Our fingers, toes and mouth are good at feeling things.

**7** Touching helps us when we cannot see.

**8** Our sense of touch helps to keep us safe.

**9** It helps us to enjoy the world.

# Index

## About this book

*I Know That!* is designed to introduce children to the process of gathering information and using reference books, one of the key skills needed to begin more formal learning at school. For this reason, each book's structure reflects the information books children will use later in their learning career – with key information in the main text and additional facts and ideas in the captions. The panels give an opportunity for further activities, ideas or discussions. The contents page and index are helpful reference guides.

The language is carefully chosen to be accessible to children just beginning to read. Illustrations support the text but also give information in their own right; active consideration and discussion of images is another key referencing skill. The main aim of the series is to build confidence – showing children how much they already know and giving them the ability to gather new information for themselves. With this in mind, the *I know that...* section at the end of the book is a simple way for children to revisit what they already know as well as what they have learnt from reading the book.